THE TEXAS RANGERS

Rangers like Captain John Wood, clad in decorative chaps to protect his legs, wear whatever they like, for there has never been an official Ranger uniform. *(Texas Department of Public Safety)*

THE TEXAS RANGERS

Larry Adler

DAVID McKAY COMPANY, INC.

NEW YORK

Library of Congress Cataloging in Publication Data

Adler, Larry, 1939-
The Texas Rangers.

Includes index.
SUMMARY: Discusses the formation of the Texas Rangers
and their roles in protecting pioneers, in the war between Texas and
Mexico, and in today's Texas.
1. Texas Rangers. 2. Frontier and pioneer life—
Texas. 3. Texas—History. [1. Texas Rangers.
2. Frontier and pioneer life—Texas. 3. Texas—History]
F391.A27   976.4   79-2085
ISBN 0-679-20980-8

1 2 3 4 5 6 7 8 9 10

Manufactured in the United States of America

To my aunts,
Beatrice, Frances, Pauline,
Ethel, and Anne

Contents

The earliest Rangers, who often camped in the wilderness, said that their only roof was the sky. (*Painting by Frederick Remington, courtesy of M. Knoedler & Co., Inc.*)

1

Origins

In 1835, the pioneers and homesteaders who had come to Texas faced two bitter enemies. To the west were fierce tribes such as the Comanches. These Native Americans glorified war, were expert marksmen with the bow and arrow, and could ride their horses more skillfully than any cavalry force in the world. In addition to their sheer love of action and fighting, the tribes had another good reason to strike and destroy the new intruders. The Native Americans wanted to stop the flow of settlers from moving into Texas and pushing them out of their homeland. So the tribes raided farms and settlements with terrifying frequency—stealing and killing.

To the south was another deadly foe, the Mexicans. In 1835, Texas was still a province that belonged to Mexico—a situation similar to the one in 1775 when our nation was still a colony that belonged to Great Britain. But just as our forefathers started a war to win independence from England in 1775, so, too, did the

Texans begin a war to win their independence from Mexico in 1835. In that year, Texas wanted all the sharpshooters, gunpower, and hard-riding horsemen it could get.

It was for this reason—a special need for extra protection—that the Rangers were authorized in late October by the Texas Council, a group who governed the state during the revolution.

The war between Texas and Mexico was short-lived; it lasted less than a year. Very few Rangers went into combat, and none were at the famous siege of the Alamo. However, the Rangers did perform an extremely useful function during the hostilities. They patrolled the western Indian frontier and did everything possible to keep the tribes from causing bloodshed. Texas had its hands full just battling the Mexicans. It didn't want another military opponent.

Even though the Rangers concentrated their efforts against the Indians, the Texans did have one famous encounter with the Mexicans. The event occurred in 1836, and it was unique in the entire history of the Rangers because it involved an adventure at sea instead of on land.

When Texas revolted, it had to protect itself against invasion along its 400 miles of seacoast on the Gulf of Mexico. The Texas Council, which created the Rangers, also created a navy to handle that job.

The Texas Navy's original little fleet of four warships was assisted by Ranger Major Isaac Burton and twenty of his mounted men, who rode along the coast keeping a lookout for Mexican transport vessels. One day in early June, while camping by a bay more than 150 miles from the Texas-Mexico border, the Rangers spotted an enemy craft at anchor. The Rangers were itching to capture it, but they obviously couldn't attack across water on horseback. So they hit on a plan. They pretended to be Mexicans and signaled the captain to send a rowboat to meet them on shore. When five unarmed, unsuspecting Mexican oarsmen landed, they found themselves staring at the guns of the Texans. The Rangers then rowed back to the vessel and took it with ease. They were pleased to discover that it was loaded with supplies for the Mexican army.

While the Rangers waited for favorable winds to sail the ship to port, two more Mexican supply crafts dropped anchor nearby. With a rifle pointed at his heart, the captain of the captured ship was forced to lure the captains of the other two vessels aboard. This done, the Rangers again had easy pickings and seized the other supply ships virtually without a fight.

Proudly, Isaac Burton and his men piloted their booty into the closest coastal town and turned everything over to their countrymen. The Ranger company gained instant fame for what it had done, and was given the appropriate and colorful nickname of "The Horse Marines."

When the revolution ended, the victorious Texans formed a republic and became a separate and distinct country detached from both Mexico and the United States. The Republic of Texas remained in existence for nine years until it eventually joined the union in 1845.

During the period of the Republic, the Rangers were called on frequently when there was trouble with the Indians or Mexicans. The volunteer soldiers who had fought for Texas during the revolution went back home to their families when the fighting ended. There

After a long gun battle, one Ranger, a man of few words, reported to his captain, "We had a little shooting match . . . and they lost." (*Texas State Library*)

The Comanche were the most feared and hated tribe in Texas, and they massacred many early settlers. (*The Museum of the American Indian, Heye Foundation*)

were very few sheriffs. And present-day defenders of citizens and the law—the National Guard, state troopers, or police, for example—did not exist in Texas back in the mid-1800s. So, the Rangers were often the only organization available for help in times of danger.

These courageous armed horsemen sometimes acted as peace officers and sometimes acted as soldiers, depending on the circumstances. That made them doubly useful to the Republic. They operated strictly as free-lancers. They worked—and were paid—only when needed. On occasion, they were enlisted for three short months of duty, then cut from the service. That kind of arrangement fitted in perfectly with the Republic's financial situation.

The Republic started out with over a million dollars in debts. Because the amount kept getting higher each year, the Republic could not afford to provide full-time patrolmen or a militia to protect its inhabitants. When the Rangers were formed, pay was set at $1.25 a day. For that amount, a recruit had to furnish his own food, clothing (the Rangers have never worn uniforms), blankets, saddle and bridle, and his own horse. Clearly, the Republic got a bargain whenever it employed the Rangers.

2

The First Famous Ranger Leader

Ranger companies were always kept limited in size by the Republic—the fewer the men, the lower the payroll. But even small groups of individuals need leaders and decision makers, and the Rangers were no exception.

Only a handful of people received appointments as Ranger officers—the best of a bold, daring lot. John Coffee Hays was one of the select few. "Jack," as he was called by his friends, rose from private to captain to colonel, and emerged as the first noteworthy head of the mounted force.

Hays wasn't a man to brag. He never was interested in publicity. "Kill 'em, let 'em lay, and say nothing," was one of his favorite slogans. Even so, under his command, the Rangers gained worldwide attention and fame, and established a reputation for bravery, spirit, and pluck that still exists to this day.

Someone said that Hays had "the courage of twenty lions," yet it wasn't just his lack of fear that made him such a great leader. Jack was a creative thinker who used his brains as well as his guns. In fact, when he thought the situation called for it, he tried psychology and persuasion against his adversaries instead of brute force.

Jack Hays was born to a wealthy family in Tennessee, in 1817. His prosperous grandfather had purchased a famous mansion from Andrew Jackson. Hays left home at fifteen, worked as a surveyor for four years, then drifted into the Republic and joined the Rangers. His talents caught the eyes of several influential Texans, and he was promoted to the rank of captain at the age of twenty-three.

Jack Hays never commanded from the rear. At the start of a battle he'd shout, "Follow me, men," and lead the charge. *(Western History Collections, University of Oklahoma Library)*

His first expeditions in his new post were against Mexican army troops and bandits, who were still seeking revenge for the loss of their province and territory. But his most exciting early clashes were against Comanche warriors in 1841 and 1842.

Hays seemed to thrive on dangerous encounters against the natives. Once he was out on a solitary scouting mission when he saw a cloud of dust far in the distance. At least ten hard-riding Indians were after him. Instantly, the captain dug his spurs into his horse and the chase was on. As he galloped toward the Ranger camp, Hays saw that the situation was hopeless. His enemies were sure to overtake him before he could reach his destination. Hays decided on a life-or-death gamble, based on his knowledge of the countryside and the intelligence of his horse. He changed direction and rode to the top of a nearby hill. Then he took cover behind a huge rock, placed all his weapons and ammunition beside him for the forthcoming gun fight, slapped his horse, and told it, "Go home!"

The captain, an excellent shot, was able to keep the Indians from closing in on him for about an hour until, for the second time that day, he saw a cloud of dust in the distance. The Rangers were coming to the rescue! His men had spotted Hays' riderless horse. Realizing that something was wrong, they had followed the animal's trail to its master.

Another time, Hays and his men were out on a mission when they spied a dozen braves. Not wanting to meet the Rangers out in the open, the Indians rode into a dense thicket. There they dismounted, ran into the woods, and hid behind some large oak trees, which gave them good defensive cover. When the Rangers

Until Hays introduced his men to the lightweight, revolving pistol, which could be fired from horseback, the Rangers fought on the ground, using heavy rifles. *(Painting by Frederick Remington, courtesy of M. Knoedler & Co., Inc.)*

surrounded the area to prevent escape, Hays and two of his men cautiously entered the thicket. Shots were fired, and Hays scrambled out with a badly wounded Ranger. The other Ranger he left behind lay dead.

Hays swore vengeance. Throwing caution to the wind and disregarding the pleas of his men, he grabbed some extra weapons and went after the Indians alone. The other Rangers waited. Three quick shots were heard, then silence. Another shot, more silence. Again and again, there was a shot and then silence, until a lone Indian fled from the woods and was brought down by a bullet.

Not knowing what they would find, the Rangers

entered the thicket. There, counting up his score, was Hays. The marksman had single-handedly dealt with eleven braves. It was no wonder that Hays was such a hero to his troops, no wonder that they would follow him into battle against overwhelming odds.

Hays' men knew that he would lead them against a larger enemy force only if he was certain of victory. And Hays felt confident that the Rangers could always lick their opponents, even when outnumbered four to one. He had equipped his men with a deadly new weapon: a destructive firearm that could swing the odds in favor of the underdog, a gun that at that time was used only by the Rangers and no other force in the world. The weapon was the revolving pistol, more popularly called a revolver. It was designed by Samuel Colt. Until Colt's invention, there was only enough storage space in most handguns for one bullet—the one to be fired when the trigger was pulled. After each shot, a new bullet had to be loaded into a weapon. This took time, something too precious to waste in a battle. Colt's first gun had a revolving cylinder with a storage space for five bullets. Later models held six bullets, hence the term "six shooter." (Every time a bullet was fired, the cylinder turned, or revolved, and moved another bullet into place, ready for immediate use.)

The benefit was a tremendous savings in loading time. Because of this, Colt was sure he had created a product with great sales appeal. So he formed a company and started manufacturing the first Colt revolvers in Paterson, New Jersey, in 1838.

Unfortunately, nobody in the East was interested in the weapon. Even the United States Army was not impressed with the revolver. The inventor, who had

Sam Colt made the first model for his revolving pistol while working as a sailor on a voyage from Boston to Calcutta. *(Gus Johnson)*

expected to grow rich with his pistol, became depressed. Business was terrible.

Fortunately for Colt, a number of his revolvers somehow reached Texas and got into the hands of Jack Hays. Captain Jack, who saw the many advantages the weapon possessed, realized how it could change the Rangers' entire approach to combat.

Before the Rangers started using the revolver, they had relied mostly on the long rifle, which had to be loaded with a new bullet after every shot. Because it was heavy and had a hard recoil, it could only be fired with accuracy by a marksman who had both legs planted firmly on solid ground. That meant that before the Colt, the Rangers had to do all their fighting while standing or kneeling on the ground.

The revolver not only held extra bullets, it was also light and easy to carry. It was a weapon the Rangers could use on horseback as well as on foot. And so, because of Colt's revolving pistol and the foresight of

This Colt six-shooter, called "The Dragoon," was manufactured in the late 1840s. *(Gus Johnson)*

Jack Hays, the Rangers became a different kind of unit than before: a force of mounted gunfighters.

This placed the utmost importance on the quality of a Ranger's mount and the abilities of the rider. Previously, a horse carried a Ranger to a scene of trouble. But now, the animal became more than just a means of transportation. A horse became an important piece of equipment on the battlefield. A Ranger's life could depend on his riding skill and the intelligence of his mount. Of necessity, Rangers became better riders than ever, and bought and broke in the smartest, fastest horses they could find.

Rangers argued about which breed was best. Some Rangers selected thoroughbred racehorses, foaled in Kentucky, or other Southern states. Some chose mustangs that were descendants of the Spanish conquistadors' horses. Others liked cow ponies, ancestors of the modern breed of quarterhorse. Yet all Rangers agreed on one thing: it was vital for them to take good care of their mounts. So Rangers' horses were fed a varied and nourishing diet of corn, grain, hay, and fresh prairie grass.

Hays placed a good deal of value on the quality and physical appearance of a Ranger's mount. In fact, when a new man came to sign up, Hays examined the volunteer's horse as carefully as the volunteer himself. Both had to measure up to the Rangers' high standards before an enlistment was offered.

When Hays first led his men into battle with their new Colt pistols, they met a war party of about eighty Comanches. Even though there were only fifteen Rangers, the Texans had two things on their side—

surprise weapons and new surprise tactics. The Comanches expected the Rangers to fight on foot with their single-shot rifles. Instead, the Texans charged on horseback with blazing guns. The Native American warriors retreated in defeat.

Soon after this skirmish, a company of twenty-five Rangers overcame another war party of approximately 100 braves. Again and again the outnumbered Rangers crushed their warrior foes, thanks to their Colts. The continuing losses were so demoralizing that several Indian chiefs agreed to sign peace treaties. For several years afterward, most tribes were so fearful of the Rangers that they shied away from open combat. Instead, the native warriors shifted their tactics to surprise hit-and-run attacks. But Hays had learned to ride the Texas plains and spot even the most difficult-to-find Indian hideouts. The trick was to look for buzzards that always flew above a tribal camp. Once Hays had found his target, he struck when the enemy was sleeping and least prepared for an onslaught.

The Comanche came to realize that whenever they made a sneak raid, they could very well expect one in return. And because of this "understanding," a short period of relative quiet developed between the two sides. But that didn't mean that Hays was kept idle. It merely meant that he could shift his attention back to the other enemy—the Mexicans. Hays did his best to stop Mexican sweeps into Texas, but he was hampered by the growing poverty of the Republic and the lack of cash for men and supplies.

His chance to lead a large company of Rangers against the Mexicans came only after Texas was admitted to statehood in 1845. At that time, the federal government claimed that all land north of the Rio Grande River belonged to Texas and, therefore, was part of America. Mexico disagreed. The Mexicans claimed that the Texas borderline was on the Nueces River, which was above the Rio Grande. The dispute over who owned what land caused the two countries to start the Mexican War in 1846. The United States Army came on the scene and mustered two regiments of Rangers into national service for six months. One of those regiments was led by Hays.

The Rangers looked forward to the conflict. The cry of "Remember the Alamo" was still in their minds. So, too, was the memory of a number of Mexican atrocities committed against fellow Texans.

The Americans rode south of the border and had their first revenge when they stopped at Reynosa, a town in which some Texans had been horribly mistreated when taken prisoner a few years before. Some of the former prisoners, who were now Rangers, recognized their tormentors, and shot them in cold blood or hanged them. News about the murderous Rangers began to spread. Soon, the Mexicans dreaded them. Even the Rangers' employer, the United States Army, became frightened of them. One general confessed that he could not control the wild Texans. "I have not the power," he wrote, "I fear they are a lawless set."

The United States Army camped at Reynosa for some time, and the idle Rangers started creating their own excitement. They held races and riding contests with stunts and tricks. They danced at fiestas, even though they were unwelcome guests. And on July 4, 1846, they celebrated Independence Day by killing and roasting some pigs and chickens, and washing the meal down with two horse buckets of whiskey.

Finally, the Army went back on the move, and the Rangers again performed their prescribed duties: carrying messages, trail-blazing routes for the Army to follow, and scouting enemy positions and movement.

Near the end of September, the Army and the Rangers arrived at a key Mexican city, Monterrey. The Army planned to stop outside the city and shell its inner defenses before attacking. But the Rangers, eager for a fight, stormed the city without waiting for the bombardment. An American general, furious at the Rangers, turned his cannons on Monterrey.

When the battle for the city was finally over, the Americans agreed to a two-week truce, and allowed the Mexicans to evacuate the city in peace. The Rangers howled in protest at this decision. They were silenced on the first day of October, when their enlistments ran out and they were sent back home. The Army didn't want the Rangers hanging around killing time—and people.

After a lengthy stalemate, the war picked up again. Without the Rangers, American soldiers suffered. Couriers were killed, lines of communication broke down, and guerilla attacks weakened the Americans' strength. Still, the Army refused to call back the uncontrollable Rangers. It took an order from the President of the United States, James Polk, to overrule the military's objections and re-enlist the Rangers. Polk personally asked for Hays' presence in the war.

In December 1847, the Rangers made a triumphant entry into Mexico City. An eyewitness wrote the following account of the event:

There arrived here recently the greatest American curiosities that have yet entered the city. They were the observed of all observers, and excited as much lively interest as if President Polk and the American Congress had suddenly set themselves down in front of the palace. Crowds of men flocked to see them (from a respectful distance, however) and women, affrighted, rushed from the balconies into their homes. Perhaps you would like to know who these terrible beings were. Well, they are nothing more or less than Jack Hays and his Texas Rangers, with their old-fashioned, maple-stock rifles lying across their saddles, the butts of two large pistols sticking out of their holsters, and a pair of Colt six-shooters belted around their waists. . . . The Mexicans believe them to be sort of semi-civilized, half-man and half-devil, with a slight mixture of lion and snapping turtle, and have a more holy terror of them than they have of the evil saint. . . .

The Rangers were called "Los Diablos Tejanos" (The Texas Devils), by the Mexico City dwellers, and Hays' men did everything to live up to their name. They drank *pulque,* a strong alcoholic beverage, threw wild parties, and left a trail of blood. A pickpocket who stole a Ranger's handkerchief was shot. Another Mexican, who threw a rock at a Texan, was gunned down. And when one Ranger was murdered in a rough section of town, the Rangers went on a rampage that left eighty Mexicans dead.

When a United States Army general called Hays in for a tongue-lashing, Hays politely told the man to mind his own business. The only person the Rangers would listen to was Hays.

17

This was proved during a very tense situation. As the Mexican War drew to a close, the United States Army captured the head of the Mexican forces—Santa Anna. Santa Anna had led the Mexicans at the siege of the Alamo during the revolution, and had murdered American prisoners during the present war. Above all others, he was the man the Rangers wanted to have in their clutches. And he was going to be passing right across their path on a safe-conduct journey, granted by the Supreme Commander of the American forces.

Four words from Hays stopped the Rangers from even touching a man they despised. Jack Hays, a master at controlling his unruly crew when he wanted to, said, "You will dishonor Texas." The Rangers reacted by letting Santa Anna pass unharmed.

As a result of the Mexican War, the Rangers became notorious in Mexico. Yet, at the same time, they also became famous throughout the United States and the rest of the world. Although they had rarely been heard of outside their own state, the Rangers gained the acclaim of American foot soldiers, and American and foreign journalists who covered the war. All praised the Rangers. Battlefield letters home, and hundreds of published articles and stories made heroes of the Texans. Thus, the Rangers' image was born and grew.

Soon after the Mexican War, Hays left the Rangers' service. Broke, almost without a penny, he hitched a ride on a prairie schooner to California, where he was made sheriff of San Francisco. He later held other government offices, and died, honored and well-to-do, in 1883. After his departure, the Rangers were almost nonexistent for ten years.

3

Good-bye, Indians

When the Mexican War was over, there was no further need for the Rangers. The federal government had taken over the problem of dealing with Native Americans when the Lone Star State joined the union.

Unfortunately, Uncle Sam's new policy toward the Indians differed from that of the Texans. The Texans had tried to push the tribes from the land, either through warfare or forced migration. The United States government tried to get the two sides to live peacefully. Soldiers were sent in to accomplish this next-to-impossible task.

The white men lived in the eastern part of Texas; the Indians in the western part. So the Army set up a string of posts the whole length of the state. After that, the Native Americans were told to stay on their side of the imaginary line formed by the posts and to leave the Texans alone.

The Indians didn't listen. Why should they have done so? There were too many suspicious, land-hungry

Texans around. So tribal warriors continued to raid. To make matters worse, it was felt that the presence of the Army encouraged the Indian assaults. The United States soldiers were reluctant to act against the tribes for any wrongdoings. The Army claimed it was in the Lone Star State to protect the Indians and promote peace, not war. But watching horse thieves and murderers go unpunished raised Texans' tempers to the boiling point. Finally, after long years of frustration, the Texans exploded.

In 1858, the Rangers were called back in force to handle the Indians the Texans' way. For about two years, there was a bloodbath. All peaceful tribes living on reservations were driven out of the state and into Oklahoma, which was then a federal Indian territory. All the remaining tribes were classified as outlaws. As such, they could be shot with no questions asked.

In late 1860, near the end of the slaughter, the Rangers took one of their most famous prisoners—a white woman named Cynthia Ann Parker. Cynthia Ann, who had been captured by the Comanches when she was still a child, had been raised by the tribe. As she grew up, various efforts were made to release her. However, every time ransom was offered, it was refused.

Cynthia Ann adopted all the ways of her captives and married the chieftain of a warrior band. She was leading the life of a Native American when the Rangers stormed her husband's camp. All the men were away hunting; only defenseless women and children were there, and they fled in panic.

The savage Texans, whose own women had been mutilated by the enemy, opened fire. Suddenly the

Cynthia Ann Parker lost her infant daughter, Prairie Flower, not long after their capture. *(Western History Collections, University of Oklahoma Library)*

wind blew a blanket away from the face of a terrified mother, running with her eighteen-month-old child. The woman had blue eyes and blond hair.

"Don't shoot her!" a Ranger screamed above the noise of the gunfire. "She's white."

Cynthia Ann was taken to a Ranger captain. She spoke no English, and it was impossible to get any information from her. Against her will, she was taken to what the Texans looked on as "civilization."

Her family welcomed her back, and the state gave

her a pension and land. It was to no avail. Cynthia Ann was used to being a Comanche. Unable to adjust to her new life, she tried to escape to the people she had been with for over twenty-four years, but was prevented from doing so. Cynthia Ann remained unhappy the rest of her life. The Parkers never considered returning her to her adopted family. Cynthia Ann's son, Quanah Parker, became a more famous chief than his father. He was the last of the Comanche leaders to surrender to the Americans.

The Civil War worked to the Indians' advantage. It gave them time to regroup and refortify themselves. And it also drained Texas of manpower when Rangers and other Texans went off to join the Confederate Army. Few ablebodied people were left to protect themselves against the Indians.

Naturally, the Comanche, Kiowa, Cheyenne, Arapaho, and other tribes took advantage of the situation. In the midst of the Civil War, the Indians went back on the warpath. And by the time the fighting hostilities between the North and South ended, the tribes had pushed back some settlers and their lines of defense as much as one hundred miles.

With the war over, the United States government again took over the administration of Indian affairs in Texas. It again brought in the Army to separate the Indians from the Texans. And it again allowed the Indians to plunder and steal.

Since the Army supposedly was protecting everyone in Texas, the Rangers were completely disbanded until 1874. By that time, officials in Washington, D.C., finally faced up to a cold hard fact. The Indians were getting away with murder. That had to be stopped once

John Jones was not a typical Ranger leader. His favorite drink was butter-milk. *(Texas State Library)*

and for all. Unfriendly tribes were going to have to be deprived of their freedom of movement and forcibly contained and restrained in reservations that, in some respects, would resemble prisons.

When the Rangers re-formed to help accomplish this task, Major John B. Jones was named as their head. The Major had the regal air of a man with complete confidence in himself and his ability to lead. In some respects, Jones was not a typical Ranger. He did not smoke and did not drink alcoholic beverages. In fact, his favorite drink was buttermilk.

Jones had a quality that all Rangers shared. He was superb in the saddle. "As a horseman, I have never seen his equal," wrote a woman friend. "His steed and himself seemed to be one—in perfect rhythm and harmony in every movement. He was simply irresistible on horseback. . . ."

Jones organized the Rangers into six companies, and all were ready to ride by July 10th. Two days later, the Major and his men had their first contact with Indians in a place aptly named Lost Valley. The Rangers were surrounded, poorly positioned, outnumbered, and without water. The group survived only because one brave Ranger volunteer risked his life to bring back a rescue party.

Jones, like other Ranger commanders, was by no means perfect. However, he made up for his initial blunder. In little more than a year, he completely cleared all the Indians out of the territory over which he ranged. The enemy finally seemed to prefer their reservations to fighting Ranger forces.

The Rangers' last long chase after a band of tribesmen was an off-again, on-again affair which started in 1879. At that time, an Apache chief escaped from a New Mexico reservation with over two hundred members of his clan. The Apaches crisscrossed the Rio Grande, between Texas and Mexico, for about a year. They were eventually cornered by the Mexican Army. However, some Apaches escaped. They decided to remain in Texas, where they raided scattered groups of individuals. Finally, the Rangers took off in pursuit. They eventually found their prey and won the gunfight that followed. To the discredit of the Rangers, they took the lives of two Indian women and two Indian children, and they fired more than 200 shots before downing one fleeing brave.

The date of the engagement, January 29, 1881, marked the last time the Rangers and Native Amer-

A murderous Apache attack on a stagecoach triggered off the last gun battle in Texas between the Rangers and a band of Indians. *(Painting by Frederick Remington, courtesy of M. Knoedler & Co., Inc.)*

icans met in combat. The last battle was fought early in the morning on top of lofty Diablo Mountain in West Texas, near the Big Bend section of the Rio Grande River. When the shooting was over, one of the Texans commented: "We had almost a boundless view from our breakfast table . . . the beauty of the scenery was only marred by man's inhumanity to man, the ghostly forms of the Indians lying around."

4

Score One for the Mexicans, One for the Rangers

In the third quarter of the 1800s, the Rangers still had to contend with a large number of Mexican trouble-makers, as well as Indian warriors. It was during this time that the Texans had two of their most famous run-ins with men from south of the border.

One skirmish was a drawn-out encounter which lasted from 1859 to 1860. The other took place within a few days in November 1875. The earlier struggle produced a number of embarrassments for the Rangers.

After the Mexican War, when the United States took possession of the territory between the Rio Grande and Nueces rivers, there were many land ownership disputes between the Mexicans and the Americans. The victorious Texans, who had their country's law on their side, deprived the Mexicans of property that the Mexicans had owned for decades. In other ways, too, Mexicans were treated as second-class citizens. This made them fighting mad. One small incident was all that was needed to trigger the Mexicans' fury.

It happened on July 13, 1859, when Juan Nepomuceno Cortinas, nicknamed "Cheno," rode into Brownsville, a town on the Texas-Mexico border. Cheno walked into a coffee shop for breakfast just as an American marshall was placing a Mexican, who had once worked for Cheno, under arrest. The Mexican was being harshly treated, and Cortinas politely asked the law officer not to be so rough. The marshall replied with an insult. Guns were drawn, and the American was shot in the shoulder. In an instant, Cheno was out the door with his former employee. Both jumped on Cheno's horse and took off for parts unknown.

Cheno Cortinas was both a desperado and a gentleman. (*Texas State Library*)

The story of Cheno Cortinas' dramatic rescue spread like wildfire among Mexicans. Here was a man who could handle his pistol, who had no fear of Americans. Here was a man who could lead the Mexicans and right the wrongs they had suffered.

After the shooting, no Texan dared to arrest Cheno, and this only added to his glamour. He was called the "Robin Hood of South Texas" and became a folk hero to Mexicans on both sides of the Rio Grande. For about two months, Cheno stayed in hiding and gathered approximately one hundred followers. Then, on September 28th, Cheno's men, the *Cortinistas,* rode into Brownsville shouting, "Viva Cheno Cortinas! Meuran los Gringos! Viva la Republica de Mexico!" (Long live Cheno Cortinas! Death to the Americans! Long live the Republic of Mexico!) Not a single American came out to challenge the invaders. "Thus was a city of two to three thousand inhabitants occupied by a band of armed bandits, a thing till now unheard of in the United States," an indignant American wrote about the event.

Finally, Cheno was persuaded to leave by his cousin and a Mexican soldier. Later, he issued a stirring proclamation that inflamed the Mexicans even further, gained Cheno more followers, and scared the Americans into fainthearted action.

The Texans united into a protective group and, dragging a cannon behind them, sought out the Mexicans. Obviously, the Americans were in no hurry to meet their foe, for they covered only seven miles in seven days. When they finally did catch up with the Cortinistas at a place called Santa Rita, the encounter was like a scene from an old comic movie. Twice the

Texans were told to charge. Twice they refused to budge. And when the firing began, the men retreated to Brownsville in headlong panic.

A journalist prepared a humorous report on the event. Referring to the men and the retreat, he wrote: "Though it had taken a week to get to Santa Rita, they made much better time in getting back. I was personally acquainted with one of the officers in that famous expedition, who, though a cripple, had frequently declared to me that he got home on that occasion in less than forty minutes!"

Cheno, too, poked good-natured fun at the Americans. He used the cannon they had left behind to fire a "good morning" wake-up greeting at 6:00 a.m. every day.

Cheno Cortinas had men, guns, and a powerless opponent, yet he acted like a saint compared to what a Ranger leader might have done in the same circumstances. After the retreat of his weak enemy, he did not harm one American man, woman, or child. He did "steal" some cattle, removing a few head from a herd, then returning the rest with payment for the ones he had taken. And he captured several United States mail bags. But after he learned the contents of the letters in the bags, he resealed them and placed the bags where they were sure to be found.

Clearly, Cheno Cortinas was a gentleman. Unfortunately, he was also an outlaw. The Texans yelled for help. The first group of Rangers that arrived on the scene was a cowardly lot. One of their first acts was to take a captured, 65-year-old Cortinista and hang him. Then the Rangers went after Cheno and lost three men in an ambush. When the Rangers made another feeble

29

attempt to get their man, they were ambushed again. They tried to surprise Cortinas in camp, but got a surprise of their own. Cortinas had left the previous week.

Finally, another more disciplined force of Rangers appeared, led by John Salmon "Rip" Ford. During his restless lifetime, Ford was not only a Ranger, but a doctor, lawyer, Civil War cavalryman, writer, senator, and mayor as well. He was well known throughout Texas, and his men were cheered when they entered Brownsville. The townspeople felt that a showdown was at hand.

However, the new Ranger force never got Cheno, although once they came very close. At the end of a losing gunfight, the heroic Cortinas was the last Mexican to leave the battlefield. He emptied his revolver, leaped on his horse, and bolted away, as three Rangers

Try as they might to surprise Cheno Cortinas and take him dead or alive, the Rangers were never able to do so. *(From the film "The Texas Rangers," courtesy of The Museum of Modern Art/Film Stills Archive)*

When Mexican outlaws rode into Texas, it always meant work for the Rangers. *(Painting by Frederick Remington, courtesy of M. Knoedler & Co., Inc.)*

took aim, fired, and missed. One bullet hit his saddle, another his gunbelt, and the third ripped some hair off his head, but Cheno Cortinas made his getaway.

The famed outlaw went on to become a general in the Mexican army and governor of a state in his country. He once even helped Rip Ford's wife, a remarkable gesture since Ford had tried to catch him on many occasions. But Cortinas was a strange mixture of good and evil. When he had the chance to make an illegal peso (or dollar), he took it. And so, some fifteen years after his first duel against the Rangers, he again became involved in crime. He met the Texans for a second time in the short Las Cuevas War. Fortunately for both the Rangers and Mexicans who participated in this war, it did not climax in bloodshed or destruction. Instead, it ended in a battle of wits and nerves. And in this case, in contrast to the earlier set-to with Cortinas, the Rangers clearly emerged the winners.

In 1875, cattle rustling was big business on both

Leander H. McNelly led thirty Rangers on a daring raid into Mexico. He made more enemies in Texas and Washington, D.C., than he did south of the border. *(Western History Collections, University of Oklahoma Library)*

sides of the Texas-Mexico border. The kingpin of one of the largest and best organized Mexican rustling operations was none other that Cheno Cortinas. Cortinas supplied the island of Cuba with stolen American cattle. He made contracts to deliver beef on the hoof to Cuban buyers, then filled the contracts by sending rustlers into Texas. The Cubans that Cortinas dealt with were as unscrupulous as he was. They knew what they were paying for and they didn't care as long as they got what they wanted. Thus, a large number of cattle were being illegally taken across the Rio Grande. The Rangers were called in to stop the stealing.

Captain Leander H. McNelly was the leader of the Rangers assigned to the job. McNelly was a frail man, with a thin, weak voice. "When he spoke we hardly breathed," said a man who served under him. "Even the horses seemed to quit swishing and stomping."

Yet McNelly was very cool under pressure, had a will of iron, and earned the love and respect of all the Rangers.

McNelly knew he was going to need a fine animal to carry him after the bandits. Dissatisfied with the horse he was riding, he stopped off at a large ranch near the rustlers' field of operations, and saw a stand-out bay named Segal.

"You want him?" the ranch head asked. And when McNelly nodded, he received the horse as a present. "I'd rather give him to you than have those bandits come and take him," the rancher said.

Segal, who had the blood of thoroughbreds in his veins, proved to be a fine horse. He was faster than all the other Rangers' mounts. And he stood still, unhitched and unafraid, whenever the captain dismounted and fought gun battles on the ground.

McNelly rode Segal to his first major meeting with Cortinas' men, and by the captain's own count, captured two hundred and sixty-five head of stolen beef cattle. Instantly word went out that the Texas Rangers

"The Rangers are riding the trail." Frequently, these words were enough to stop Mexican cattle rustlers from staging raids into Texas. *(From the film, "The Texas Rangers," The Museum of Modern Art/Film Stills Archive)*

were on the trail. Because this was enough to stop most Mexicans from crossing the border, rustling decreased for a few months. Then Cortinas, who had a huge order to fill, sent his men back into Texas. They returned with a herd of two hundred.

McNelly had to get back into action. A United States cavalry force, based near the Texas-Mexico border, was sent to help him. In mid-November, the soldiers got an early warning about a rustling scheme. Through spies, they were told that in a few days some stolen Texas cattle would be driven across the Rio Grande and taken a few miles to a large ranch and hideout called Las Cuevas.

Because of some unnecessary waiting, the cavalry moved too late. By the time the mounted soldiers had hit their target point on the American side of the river, most of the thieves and cattle were in Mexico. The Army refused to give chase. If the soldiers moved across the river and south of the border, the incident might be considered an armed invasion of a peaceful, neighboring country. This would create an international incident and lead to complications. From the point of view of the Army commander, it wasn't worth the trouble.

Then McNelly rode into the Army camp. Due to a communications mix-up, McNelly and the Rangers had received little advance word about the cattle crossing. The captain listened to all that had happened and then made a decision that sent shock waves all the way to Washington, D. C. He would, if necessary, take his Rangers into Mexico and straight to the Las Cuevas ranch. McNelly wanted to capture stolen American cattle, and he didn't care where he had to go to do it.

What about the fact that McNelly had only thirty Rangers and that there were about fifteen times that many Mexicans at Las Cuevas? "We are going if we never come back," McNelly said.

Was he figuring on a suicide mission? Hardly. McNelly reasoned that United States troops would not stand idle while their countrymen were being shot at. So at 1:00 a.m., under a bright moon, the first Rangers started to row across the Rio Grande in a tiny, leaky boat. A few horses swam to the other side.

McNelly's audacious plan was to storm the Las Cuevas Ranch at daybreak, catch the Mexicans while they were still sleeping, and barricade himself and his men in a house until help in the form of the United States Army arrived.

While it was still dark, McNelly's men attacked and took the ranch—the wrong ranch. They had gone to a small place half a mile from Las Cuevas. That put the Rangers in a spot, for the noise of their guns removed any chance of a surprise attack on their foe.

But McNelly didn't go back. He went on. And only when he saw the size and readiness of the Las Cuevas force did he order the Rangers to retreat. The Mexicans came hunting, ready to wipe out the whole Ranger bunch.

McNelly, now running away from the bandits, had not taken back one head of stolen cattle. Furthermore, if he retreated to the American side, he would lose all hope of capturing any American stock. Despite the seemingly hopeless situation, McNelly's mind kept turning. When he hit the Rio Grande, he planted his Rangers on the Mexican side of the river.

On came the Mexicans.

"Randlett, for God's sake, come over and help us!" McNelly shouted to an officer on the other side of the Rio Grande.

Randlett responded to the cry. American troops were ordered into Mexico.

Now, with shooting going on all around him, the wily McNelly kept cool, and tried to talk Randlett into attacking Las Cuevas. Randlett, of course, refused.

Both sides ceased firing for a while. During the lull, the Mexicans produced a white flag. An emissary came out to meet McNelly. When he asked the captain to leave Mexican soil, McNelly said, "No." He wanted the cattle he had come for.

The cease-fire continued, and a long standoff developed. The Mexicans and Rangers acted like two boxers in the opening round of a fight, feinting, parrying, and testing each other without ever throwing a punch. The Mexicans refused to surrender their stolen stock, McNelly refused to move his men. He did not even appear outwardly disturbed when the United States Army pulled back across the Rio Grande, leaving the Rangers all by themselves.

During the night of November 19th, 30 Texans camped near about 500 Mexicans with only a flag of truce between them. The following day, the telegraph wires between Texas and the nation's capital were burning with messages. McNelly was put under great pressure. He was told that the Army now had clear orders not to help him if he remained in Mexico. When he received a message to retreat by order of the Secretary of War, he replied, "I shall remain in Mexico with my rangers . . . and shall recross the Rio Grande at my own discretion. Give my compliments to the Secretary of War and tell him the United States troops may go to hell."

Meanwhile, the Mexicans waited. They had no idea what was going on. They saw that the Rangers were in one place, the United States Army in another. They also saw a number of important-looking telegrams and messages passed back and forth between the Texans and the soldiers. The Mexicans did not know that McNelly was powerless. They thought that perhaps the Army was getting ready to invade. The tension increased. McNelly and the Rangers remained strong and determined. The Mexicans wilted. They finally decided to give in.

Seventy-five head of cattle were returned to the American side of the Rio Grande. It was the first time in Texas history that stolen cattle had been reclaimed from Mexico, and the event caught everyone's attention and interest. That was just what McNelly wanted. Cattle rustling across the border dropped to nearly zero. The Rangers' mission was a complete success.

A year after the Las Cuevas War, Cheno Cortinas was placed under house arrest by a new president of Mexico. Cortinas did no harm after that. As for McNelly, he had stepped on too many toes and made too many politicians angry. In 1877, his enemies used his poor health as an excuse to have him fired. He died the same year.

McNelly's deeds were celebrated in a saying that goes:

> When the Texas Rangers' hoof-beats thunder along the border, two nations tremble.
> The United States does not know where they will stop.
> Mexico does not know what can stop them.

5

The New Enemies

As mentioned before, the Rangers fought their last gun battle against the Indians in early 1881. Around that time, lawless Mexicans, such as Cheno Cortinas, operated mostly along a narrow strip by the Rio Grande River. But that did not mean that the Rangers in the rest of the state could relax when the Indian troubles were drawing to a close. In fact, the Rangers were overburdened with work from the mid-1870s to the early 1880s. Their new enemies were their fellow Texans—outlaw, gunslingers, and killers, who committed more crimes than ever during the Reconstruction period that followed the Civil War. During that time, there were a number of social and economic upheavals that led to a breakdown in law and order throughout the Lone Star State.

Confederate soldiers, returning from the battlefield, brought back a "war mentality" that stressed bloodshed. As a result, there was an increase in gunplay and shootings. Texans rebelled against the laws of their state, due to the "carpetbaggers"—corrupt Northerners who ran Texas until normal peacetime conditions could be restored. The feeling was that if government officers openly broke the law, why shouldn't everybody else?

Rival families or political groups started violent feuds. Sometimes one side "bought" a sheriff or threatened a judge, jury member, or witness. It often became imposssible to seek or obtain justice.

Roving, armed gangs sometimes took over towns and terrorized the inhabitants. Bandits began to have more targets to rob because more banks were opened, more stagecoaches started rolling and more railroads were built. Rustling became widespread throughout the state as cattle ranching became increasingly profitable.

The Rangers' best-known enemies during those times were desperadoes such as Sam Bass and John Wesley Hardin. These men were glorified by the newspapers and magazines of their day. Legends grew up about them, and they were celebrated in both folklore and song.

Sam Bass was especially popular during his reign as an outlaw. Known as "Texas' Beloved Bandit," he appealed to many Texans because he specialized in robbing banks. Average citizens, who felt that they were being cheated by the banks, were glad to hear that the banks were being robbed in return by Sam Bass. The outlaw, who also made the biggest train hauls of his time, had a sentimental side. He returned $20 to a one-armed passenger during a train robbery, and he used his six-gun only as a last resort. He was able to outwit a horde of Pinkerton detectives and

A lone stagecoach, carrying passengers and valuable cargo, made a tempting target for bandits. *(Painting by Frederick Remington, courtesy of M. Knoedler & Co., Inc.)*

bounty hunters who were chasing after him. But unfortunately for Bass, when all other searchers failed, the Rangers were called in. They got their man.

Sam Bass, who hailed from Mitchell, Indiana, came to Denton, Texas, in 1870. For a few years he worked, saved his money, and lived a quiet and respectable life. Then, in 1874, Sam bought a little sorrel mare called Jenny. The horse was better known as "the Denton mare" in a famous ballad about the bandit. A great racehorse, the mare won a bundle for Sam and turned him into a gambler.

Sam had "wanderlust" for a while, traveled north, and wound up staging robberies in South Dakota and Nebraska. After a big holdup that netted him $10,000, Sam went back to Denton. He spent lavishly until his funds were low again. Then he returned to his former "occupation."

At the height of Sam's activity, the Rangers were ordered to get on his trail. The Rangers planted a spy in Sam's midst, a man Bass trusted because of his help in the past. The spy informed the Rangers of Bass' plans to rob the bank at Round Rock, Texas. So when Bass and two of his followers rode into town, the Rangers were ready and waiting. In the gunfight that followed, one accomplice was killed, and Sam was hit by two bullets. The other brave bandit held off the Rangers, backed into an alley, unhitched two horses, lifted his leader into the saddle, and rode off with the mortally wounded man.

The next day, Sam Bass was found sitting under a tree a few miles out of town. The outlaw, who realized he was dying, had told his associate to ride off and save himself. Bass lingered for a few days, but steadfastly

There was a sharp rise in saloon and gambling hall gun-fights after the Civil War, when the Rangers pursued more killers than ever. *(Painting by Frederick Remington, courtesy of M. Knoedler & Co., Inc.)*

refused to squeal on his past or present comrades because, as he put it, "It's agin' my profession."

John Wesley Hardin, another criminal sought by the Rangers, was a completely different person from Bass. A family man who adored his wife and children, he was extremely intelligent and even wrote a book about his life. However, unlike Bass, Hardin was a vicious, bloodthirsty killer. There was no one at his side to keep count, but Hardin is said to have murdered at least twenty-five men, and perhaps as many as forty.

The son of a preacher, Hardin was fascinated with guns as a child. He became an expert with the Colt .45, and at sixteen, he had a reputation for being one of the deadliest gunfighters in Texas.

Oddly enough, Hardin was also a diligent student in his youth. One time, by a hideout campfire, he studied for an exam given by an unsuspecting tutor at a private academy. And Hardin, himself, worked as a substitute teacher while he was still a teenager.

On May 26, 1874, Hardin was celebrating his twenty-first birthday in a Texas saloon when a deputy tried to outdraw and shoot him. Hardin had his back to the deputy. But because of some sixth sense, Hardin spun around, drew, and fired before the other man's gun was clear of his holster. It was obviously a case of self-defense, but because of Hardin's previous crimes, the state put a price on his head. The outlaw lay low for three years. He fled to Alabama, where he was joined by his wife and family, and where he became a partner in a prosperous logging business.

Eventually, the Rangers were tipped off as to Hardin's whereabouts. They came running, spurred on by the fat reward offered for his capture. Although the Rangers did not normally pursue criminals outside Texas, they made an exception in Hardin's case because a large reward was offered for his return.

The Rangers trailed Hardin to Pensacola, Florida, where he went to buy supplies for his business. There, in a railroad carriage, Hardin was jumped by some Rangers and local law officials. After the unequal struggle, Hardin remained calm, insisted on his alias (a false name he was using), and protested that the Texans had the wrong man.

When a Ranger threatened to blow Hardin's brains out, the outlaw coolly replied, "Blow away. You will never blow a more innocent man's out." When another Ranger called him "John Wesley Hardin," the bandit asked, "Stranger, what asylum are you from?"

However, the Texans were not fast-talked into letting Hardin go. John Wesley Hardin spent nineteen

Fearless and quick on the trigger, the Rangers had an uncanny skill with firearms. *(Painting by Frederick Remington, courtesy of M. Knoedler & Co., Inc.)*

long years in jail, studied law, and emerged an attorney. His faithful wife, who had waited so long for his release, died a year before he was freed. Once out of prison, Hardin shied away from gun-happy kids. But he couldn't escape his past. He met his end when he was shot in a saloon.

Whenever the Rangers captured a man like Hardin or Bass, they created more uneasiness than ever among the other criminals they were after. It seemed as if there was no way to escape the pursuing Rangers. A suspect could easily talk himself into surrendering, and often the decision to give up was based on more than just a fear of the Rangers.

The Rangers protected the men they captured until a fair trial could be arranged and completed. This was extremely important in certain situations. An apprehended man might have armed enemies, or he might be accused of a particularly horrible crime that aroused the violent passions of the local inhabitants. In those cases, it was not uncommon for a crowd to storm a local jail, overpower the sheriff, and hang the unfortunate accused.

The Rangers did not want those kinds of embarrassing incidents happening to their suspects. The Rangers' job was to uphold the law, and the law said that every man was entitled to his day in court, no matter how hideous his supposed crime or how strong the evidence was against him. So the Rangers made sure their captives were kept safe and secure.

In one instance, an armed mob threatened to tear down a jail to get at a particularly hated prisoner taken by the Rangers. A courageous officer stood in front of the screaming, cursing crowd and sent them home with this short, droll warning: "Do not tear down the jail, gentlemen. You have been taxed for years to build this fine structure—it is yours—do not tear it down. I

In 1890, these four Rangers posed at a remote place called Basque Bonito. *(Texas Department of Public Safety)*

will open the doors wide—you can all come in—do not tear down the jail, but there are twelve Rangers in there, with orders to kill as long as they can see. Come right in, gentlemen—but come fixed."

To tackle their job in a better organized manner, the Rangers compiled a book, *A List of Fugitives from Justice*. It was nicknamed "The Ranger's Bible," and it was studied by every member of the force. Included in its more than 200 pages were notations about thousands of wanted men. The Rangers, who memorized descriptions of those criminals, had enormous success in capturing them. Many who were never caught remained free only because they fled the Lone Star State.

The only kind of criminal who wasn't intimidated by the Rangers was the gang leader. A gang leader—usually the head of a cattle ranch—might control 100 or more gunslingers. With so many killers on his payroll, the head of an outlaw band could easily bully a city full of innocent people. Factors such as these combined to give a gang leader a great sense of security and power.

King Fisher was the boss of one of the most ruthless gangs in Texas. Once employed as a gunman for other cattle owners, Fisher later became a rancher. He hired a band of armed and dangerous cowboys to work for him, and soon he was the ruler of the territory around Eagle Rock, just north of the Rio Grande.

Fisher's word became law. Nobody opposed him. His men stole cattle in broad daylight. The local judge went into hiding. The entire Eagle Rock community lived in mortal terror of King Fisher's band.

Finally, the Texas Rangers came to Fisher's ranch to arrest him and some of his men. Fisher surrendered with a smile. With his might and influence, he knew he

Rangers Brown and White pose on their respective mounts, Buckskin and Old Sorrell, in Presidio County, Texas. *(Texas Department of Public Safety)*

could wiggle out of whatever charges were being placed against him. And sure enough, the authorities turned King Fisher loose. "You could not persuade a man in this whole country to testify against King Fisher or any of his clan," one Texan wrote.

The Rangers kept up the pressure, however. They listened to eyewitnesses to the cattle rancher's crimes, and they promised protection to members of a grand jury. A year later, in 1877, they arrested Fisher again. This time, the Rangers jailed him in San Antonio, which they thought was outside King Fisher's sphere of influence. Unfortunately, the Rangers were wrong. Despite twenty-one indictments, and six consecutive jury trials, Fisher was never convicted of a single crime. He laughed in the Rangers' faces, and went back to his cattle and crime. The Texans could only stand by, helpless and disappointed.

Surprisingly, Fisher eventually reformed. He married, raised a family, and—of all things—became a peace officer himself.

King Fisher was by no means the only Texas cattleman who came into conflict with the Rangers. However, many of the other lawbreaking ranchers were not desperate outlaws or even rustlers. Their crime was trying to keep the Texas range wide open and free.

From the end of the Civil War to the start of this century, millions of heads of Texas longhorns were herded on long drives from the heart of the Lone Star State to shipping points and markets in the midwest. When these drives first began, there were few fences in Texas cattle country. No fencing material existed that could bar the path of a thundering herd of cattle, so they were able to roam anywhere, to graze wherever there was grass, and to quench their thirst wherever there was water. Naturally, this limited the spread of farming. Surprisingly, the open range also was harmful to cattlemen with the most money and best land. If a rich rancher bought an expensive stud bull to improve his herd, he couldn't stop the animal from breeding with another rancher's cow. If a rich rancher owned prime acreage, he couldn't stop another man's stock from feeding and drinking on his property.

Then barbed wire was created in 1873. The barbs pricked the hide of cattle, stopped the animals in their tracks, and kept them enclosed within the fenced areas. A revolution occurred. With barbed wire, a rancher or farmer could section off his land for his own private use. Naturally, the wealthiest Texans bought barbed wire first.

Phot By G H Walker

This Ranger company, led by Captain Jerry Grey (second from left), was stationed in Marfa, in west Texas, in 1918. (*Texas Department of Public Safety*)

When the poorer, smaller "free grass" ranchers responded to the situation by illegal fence cutting, in came the Rangers. Their task was to catch cutters in the act.

The Rangers didn't like sitting by a fence all night, waiting for a cutter to appear. It was dull, boring, unexciting—a far cry from their usual assignments. However, despite complaints, the Rangers did their job. Gradually, the fence war diminished. In the end, the fence cutters realized that, "if you can't beat 'em, join 'em." They, too, set up their own fences.

Soon, a huge area of Texas was sectioned off by fences—a foreboding sign of the end of the old frontier days.

6

Still Going Strong

The closing of the frontier meant that all of Texas was settled. More people than ever were thronging to the state. They built homes in the areas where Indians and bandits used to roam. They moved into Texas' cities, making the communities larger, richer, and more modern. As the state prospered, the legal system and police force gained more power and began to function more efficiently and effectively. Individuals put away the

The modern Ranger still has to be a good horseman and an expert marksman. *(Texas Department of Public Safety)*

Because cattle are still rustled in Texas, Rangers still have to check brand to establish ownership. *(Texas Department of Public Safety)*

guns they used to holster, for there was no longer a need to carry them. The crimes associated with a frontier society—shoot-outs, stagecoach robberies, and cattle rustling—either lessened or stopped completely. Texas had entered a new era, and so had the Rangers.

They were still called on when the authorities needed their help. But as the nineteenth century drew to a close and the twentieth century emerged, the Rangers were asked to perform new assignments that differed from their previous tasks. In 1896, the Rangers stopped an illegal boxing match from being fought on

Texas soil. In 1899, during a smallpox epidemic along the Rio Grande, they forced unwilling Mexicans to get vaccinated and obey the quarantine. In 1900, they acted as escorts for strikebreakers. When World War I started, they were called in to catch German spies and sympathizers, and men who dodged the draft. And in the 1920s and early 1930s, the Rangers helped enforce Prohibition.

In 1935, the Rangers merged with the Texas State Highway Patrol, run by the newly created Department of Public Safety.

Texas Rangers have encountered many new kinds of criminals in the twentieth century, including safecrackers. (*Texas Department of Public Safety*)

Even Texas Rangers take coffee breaks. *(Texas Department of Public Safety)*

Since then, Rangers have continued to perform a wide variety of duties. They have assisted communities during times of disaster, quelled disturbances over forced school integration, quashed prison riots, and stemmed the flow of illegal narcotics and drugs into the state. However, the Rangers still investigate crimes, apprehend fugitives, and protect life and property.

Today, the Rangers consist of a force of approximately 100 men, divided into six law enforcement districts. Applicants for the Ranger service must be between 30 and 50, United States citizens, in good

The horse is no longer the Rangers' only means of transportation. *(Texas Department of Public Safety)*

physical health, and have at least eight years of experience with an agency that investigates crime. The hours are long, the pay fairly low, and the work sometimes dangerous, but there is still a long waiting list for available openings.

Perhaps this is because there is still a special kind of honor attached to the job. The Rangers were, and still are, a special force. The traditions, legends, and spirit established by Hays, Ford, Jones, McNelly and other Ranger leaders are as strong today as ever before.

Index